I0116635

Life Sights™

INSIGHTS INTO THE INDIVIDUAL CHRISTIAN LIFE

Book One

The Paths to Individual Breakdown

T. George Homsher

Acknowledgments

To God the Father, God the Son and God the Holy Spirit for my eternal life and my abundant life here on earth.

I want to give wonderful appreciation to Howard Blandau for his love, his encouragement of my discipleship in the Lord Jesus, and all of his incredible insights.

I am deeply grateful to my dear wife Denise for her incredible initial editing, ongoing sacrifices and support.

I thank my dear daughter Bethany for giving me the okay to write this book (and any others that follow.) As a home-school dad and a house husband for many years I needed her consent. She said, knowing how much it would mean to me, "Dad, you can write the book."

Finally, a book of quality must have experts to provide the special brushstrokes needed to take it to another level. To that end, I sincerely thank Melissa Hardin for her excellent editing, and Victoria Robinette Merkel for her high-quality book design and composition work.

Contents

T. George Homsher
LifeSights: Book One – *The Paths to Individual Breakdown*
Copyright © 2010 T. George Homsher
All rights reserved
ISBN 978-0-9829736-0-8

Book Cover and Composition by Robinette Creative Services
Book Editing by Melissa Hardin
Published by Unto Jesus Not Men, LLC
www.untojesusnotmen.com

Preface

I met the Jesus Christ-centered counselor and psychologist Howard Blandau (pronounced BLAN-doe) when he was 62 years old. I was 23 and was immediately struck by Howard's dynamic joy, peace and strength. As the years have passed, I can say Howard Blandau is the greatest Christian man I have ever met. This book, and the ones that follow in the series, are the LifeSights of what Howard and I have seen in the lives of individual Christians, as well as in our own lives. Howard gave me full consent to write or present material in a way that brings together his thoughts and insights with mine, thus making them my own. In other words, I could write a book or present material without the heavy labor and confusion of separately documenting Howard's insights and mine. As a result, I have come to realize that this book has been written in the most dynamic and simplistic way; the way we both wanted.

When Howard was alive, I asked him why he wasn't writing a book on his incredible Christian insights and general insights that he had learned along the way. His response was that he did not have the time or the confidence to write. What is remarkable about his lack of confidence in his writing is that Howard was one of the greatest letter writers I have ever read. I now believe it was God the Father's will for me and not for Howard to write this book. It took some soul-searching and careful thought about the past to come to this conclusion.

I met Howard at the Professional Counseling Center in 1987. In the next year, he asked me to join his ministry as a professional Christ-centered counselor. I excitedly signed up for the job. Some time later, we discussed my taking over of his ministry. His main office was in Fort Washington, Pennsylvania, but he had also established offices in other parts of Pennsylvania and in New Jersey. However, as time progressed with my own Christ-centered counseling ministry in Western, Pennsylvania, it became apparent that it was not God's will for me to continue as a Christian counselor.

I had been the last Christ-centered counselor Howard had supervised at the Professional Counseling Center, as well as the last person that Howard had discipled in the Lord Jesus Christ. For many months after I left the counseling ministry, Howard continued to disciple me in Jesus and our father-son relationship continued until his passing. During our many years together, I absorbed the full maturity of Howard's insights and thoughts into the Christian and non-Christian individual's life. It must also be noted that the Professional Counseling Center that Howard founded and directed is no longer operating. However, what was born out of that great ministry is this book and God willing, the others that will follow.

In the years that followed my departure from the Professional Counseling Center, I gained a clear vision of what God the Father's will for my professional life was to be—it was for me to write or present material that God had not yet wanted Howard to write. Here are some of the reasons I believe now is the time for LifeSights:

1. God wanted Howard to concentrate on becoming the greatest Christ-centered counselor/psychologist he could be. Howard's focus on accomplishing this was staggering. He had over 100,000 hours of direct counseling with individuals, couples and families. This number of direct counseling hours is unheard of in the Helping Profession. He was on the front lines of his profession like few have been. His greatest gift was helping others in the counseling setting. In this setting, God used him in mighty ways to help others. If Howard had become a writer he would have been sidetracked from this incredible accomplishment.

2. As I reflect upon my own situation, my greatest gift in helping others is in the written or spoken form rather than helping others in the counseling setting. As I was growing up I loved writing and listening to the radio.

3. I believe it is the will of God that I present LifeSights to a broader audience. I believe there's a Christian world outside of Christian counseling that is hungering for these insights. With the spiritual breakdown of many churches it is apparent that many Christians are not being spiritually fed.

4. I also believe that it is God's desire that I write this book because Howard helped save my life. His counsel and dedication to disciple me in the Lord Jesus gave me the courage I needed to face and deal with my own negative background and shortcomings. Howard said that I could really help people because I had a unique understanding

of the insecurity and struggle of others due to my own experience and difficulties that had left me insecure and struggling. Now, it is my turn to help those who are in a similar position. I hope those who are struggling can have hope in my example as someone who has gone from a struggling Christian to someone who has come to live the abundant and victorious Christian life.

Although there are many insights from our LifeSights in this book and the ones that follow, this simple insight that Howard taught me is most important of all. It is in important sequence with an emphasis to the Holy Spirit, to the Lord Jesus and to God the Father:

- Be dependent on the Holy Spirit.
- Be relationally close to the Lord Jesus Christ.
- Be in praise, worship, glory, honor and thanksgiving to God the Father.

Unto Jesus not men,

George™

T. George Homsher

The Paths to
Individual Breakdown

Introduction

The following is a kind of roadmap for the Christian individual to understand the process of an emotional breakdown and to bring hope and understanding to this serious topic. If you understand and deal with the paths to individual breakdown, you may be able to prevent, or lessen the effects of a breakdown.

The roadmap presents the First Path and the Second Path. The discussion of the Second Path is longer, in part, because many Christians are living their lives in this direction. This is an ongoing lifestyle that many are not fully aware of, or how to get out of. This analysis can help discern where you are and what you need to do to get off the path.

Before breaking down the First and Second Paths, it is important to discuss how the two general personality types handle the paths and use of psychopharmacological medication.

THE TWO INDIVIDUAL PERSONALITIES AND HOW THEY FACE THE PATHS

The insightful emotional personality will become much more emotional when he or she faces both paths. Many times this heightened emotion will motivate them to own their own emotions or get help through counseling. Because of their heightened emotions they will tend to believe they are much worse off than they probably are. For example, the insightful emotional personality could believe he is going to have a breakdown even when he is not really close to it. If the person who has this personality can weather the early storm of heightened emotion, he can face and deal with the path(s) to intervene fairly quickly.

On the other hand, the pragmatic, less emotional individual personality will be less emotional when they face the onset of one of the individual paths. This lack of realistic emotion can cause them to believe that they do not need to take ownership and deal with their own emotions or get help through counseling. Pragmatic individuals often find themselves in serious emotional and psychological trouble because they were unaware and lacking insight into the escalating trouble that was building within. Due to this lack of insight and the newly developed and perplexing buildup of emotions, the pragmatic individual tends to believe a counselor could not help them; that they have gone too far down the path and their options are severely limited.

A General Understanding of Psychopharmacological Medication

It is usually best for anyone to begin the healing process with a psychologist, a counselor, a psychotherapist or a qualified trained pastor. I believe the non-medical, trained counseling "helper" will be more objective in determining the need to have psychopharmacological medication, as opposed to a psychiatrist, medical doctor or other medical field professional.

This is because of the growing and inaccurate belief in the medical field that certain heightened emotional or negative psychological experiences are caused by the person's own physiology. While some individuals will need psychopharmacological medication, especially in the later stages of the second path, most people will not need medication.

It is also important to understand the concern with psychopharmacological medications that, if used for an extended period of time, an individual's brain chemistry will change negatively, possibly for the rest of his or her life. The extended period of time depends on the genetic makeup of the person. Therefore, the use of extremely powerful psychopharmacological medication should be a last resort.

THE TWO MAJOR PATHS TO INDIVIDUAL BREAKDOWN

The First Path

The First Path to individual breakdown may occur when you begin to face several very difficult situations or experiences. For example: a job loss followed by a divorce. One of these experiences is difficult enough, but these two experiences combined in someone's life are extremely traumatic. If you do not know how to deal with the emotional, psychological, physical or spiritual issues surrounding difficult experiences, it could lead to a breakdown.

In this First Path, you could be dealing with things that are not in your control to change or are not your fault. Jesus Christ-centered counseling assists in facing the hurt and the anxiety that can be often overwhelming in difficult circumstances. If you choose not to get help, you will need to learn and/or implement quickly how to effectively deal with those emotions that many times begin to escalate and deepen rather quickly. Many people have decided not to get counseling or have not dealt with their inward trauma and have paid a heavy price in doing so.

The person who gets help from a quality counselor or deals with their inward trauma themselves on this First Path will have a very good chance of successfully working through these difficult situations, the heavy emotions and the psychological negativity that go with them.

The Second Path

The reason why the bulk of the analysis will be on the Christian's Second Path to individual breakdown is because it is much more complicated than the First Path. On the Second Path there is much more involved than just situations or experiences that are too overwhelming to bear. On this path, individuals have much more ability to change what they are going through because much of it is of their own doing. This is very different than the First Path where one needed to cope with, take ownership of, and deal with what had come upon them.

The Second Path is presented in stages that occur in the course of time. It is vital to understand that at each stage, all of the previous stages are building on top of the other, so one is not just experiencing the current stage, or the stage one has just come from, but many or all of the entire previous stages. This makes each succeeding stage significantly worse than the previous stage.

The Nine Stages

The Second Path has nine stages. The further along these nine stages, the harder it becomes to take responsibility in getting oneself off the path. It is best to deal with the Second Path in the early stages because each stage has a life of its own and the deep problems that go along with it. The inability to take ownership of a current stage always leads to the start of the next stage.

If a person has progressed to stage five, he will first need to deal with stage five and then take ownership and deal with stages one through four. With this in mind, it can be said that the stages begin to pile up. However, with regard to the initial stages, there is plenty of hope to turn things around even at later stages. When someone doesn't see the path to breakdown, they are more prone to get on and stay on it. This is a roadmap to give insight and the strength that comes from the knowledge that our Christian life of love, joy and peace was meant to be lived off this path.

Chapter 1

Stage One:
Heart of the Problem

Much of the secular and Christian "helping communities" are focused on the symptoms, instead of the heart of the problem, when it comes to the Second Path to individual breakdown. They may focus on anger as the heart of the problem when it really is a symptom of the basic problem (hurts or anxiety/fear). Unfortunately, there is a segment in the Christian counseling community that focuses on anger as a sin when an outwardly angry client comes to counseling. They do not see that the initial problem that caused the anger may have started without sin involved in the client's life. It is true that anger causes depression, but the heart of the problem leads to anger and that problem must be addressed to get off the path to breakdown.

During the course of a lifetime, we will all experience an abundance of hurt and anxiety. These experiences normally happen intermittently and we must be prepared to own them and handle them when they happen. It is one of many things that fall under the umbrella of the following phrase: "If you don't deal with life—life will deal with you." If we do not, there will be many tough times ahead and maybe tragic times ahead as well.

If we do own and resolve the hurts and fears in our lives, we will have a much greater possibility of having a happy, joyful, peaceful and loving Christian life. However, the tendency for us, even as Christians, is to rebel against facing and dealing with this heart of the problem, which can easily steer us into stage two.

OVERCOMING STAGE ONE

Ask the Lord Jesus to heal our hurt – When we ask the Lord for healing, we're taking ownership of our hurt and allowing Him to love us. The world can only temporarily try to heal us, that is why non-Christians never get relief from hurt on a permanent basis. This is why so many look to numb the pain because they never get a long-lasting, thorough healing from the ache. It is true there may be some hurts in life that will be with us on some level for the rest of our lives. However, the Lord will give full relief from the extreme hurt in those most painful or hurtful areas within us. Jesus is the great Healer, and He will heal us.

Ask the Lord to strengthen you and help you walk when you are fearful – When we ask Jesus to do this He and the Holy Spirit will supernaturally strengthen us and help us to face our fear. Many times in facing our fear we will experience the Lord's presence and relational closeness in our lives like never before.

When dealing with anxiety, take ownership of it as soon as possible – As the saying goes, "It's best to get back up on the horse right after you've fallen off." Many times hurt or anxiety will have to be fully felt and accepted multiple times. As we face and deal with anxiety, it helps avoid the painful consequences that come when we avoid the self-responsibility to handle our hurts and fears.

Deal with panic attacks – A growing number of Christians are experiencing the terrible fear of a heart-pounding panic attack. Someone experiencing their first panic attack can easily slip into bondage or control by their fear, but that is the critical time to take ownership of fear and address what caused the panic attack (Romans 8:15). This feeling can come from experiences such as too much stress, the inability to take self-control or a traumatic experience. For example, when a Christian lives a double life o a sinful lifestyle mixed with a Christian lifestyle, this creates enormous guilt and the heightened anxiety.

Discuss your hurt and anxiety with whomever is causing it – It is sometimes appropriate to discuss your disappointment with someone who has caused it. Note that the word "hurt" and the word "disappointed" are too different approaches. You might say, "I am disappointed at the way you spoke to me the other day." Not "I am hurt because of the way you spoke to me the other day." Labeling the emotion this way preserves your self-esteem while still courageously addressing the issue. A strong feeling of self will allow you to clarify the issue and perhaps offer forgiveness if it is needed

It is not mandatory to talk to everyone who hurts us or causes fear in our lives. If you have a close relationship to the Trinity, you will understand how to deal with difficult situations like whether to talk or not talk to someone else. Depend on the Holy Spirit. Be relationally close to the Lord Jesus, and honor, glorify and worship God the Father.

Music can be a powerful tool for healing – If you are having difficulty acknowledging your hurt or fear, the right kind of music will help to focus and feel these emotions. Soft instrumental, praise music and easy listening are recommended.

Forgive God – If your hurt or anxiety was caused by outside circumstances, you may find it difficult to pray. Cry out to Him that you have forgiven Him for allowing it to happen.

Chapter 2

Stage Two:
The Buildup of Bitterness
or Resentment

Inability to accept and work through the heart of the problem leads to the second stage. As mentioned in the first chapter, each stage carries with it the previous stage.

Many times, sin is not involved when hurt and anxiety enter our lives. It's as if God has given us a chance to avoid sin by allowing hurts or anxiety to help us wake up. However, if we do not deal with hurt and anxiety, then it is inevitable for them to become a foundation for sin in our Christian life. The door opens for sin to enter into the Second Path. This is because there is a limit to the growth and depth of hurt and anxiety and eventually, bitterness or resentment springs up. Many feel a sense of bewilderment from bitterness or resentment and question themselves on why they are feeling this way. Many run away or avoid dealing with the bitterness or resentment.

As Hebrews chapter 12:15 reveals, *"Looking diligently lest any man fail of the grace of God; lest any root of bitterness springing up trouble you, and thereby many be defiled;"*

The term bitterness means being forced to swallow something very unpleasant. It creates a lower level of unrighteous anger or an intense sense of frustration. The term resentment refers to the belief that one has experienced something negative, which he or she should not have had to experience. It also creates a lower level of unrighteous anger or an intense sense of frustration.

Instead of the individual responding to the hurt or fear with empathy or courage, the individual, who now lacks self-control, reacts to hurt or anxiety with bitterness or resentment. These are reactionary emotions and not responding emotions. As Christians, we need to respond to difficult experiences in our lives, and not react to them. Responding with empathy or courage will avoid the pitfall of bitterness and resentment.

OVERCOMING STAGE TWO

Take ownership of sin and seek forgiveness from the Lord Jesus – This ownership will be accompanied by some sorrow and a bit of regret. Not taking ownership opens the door to a double life that will lead to a more serious escalation of emotions and psychological negativity. James 3:14 says, *"But if ye have bitter envying and strife in your hearts, glory not, and lie not against the truth."*

Forgive yourself for being caught up in sin – Once forgiveness is experienced it is essential to move on from this situation as quickly as possible. The devil or even one's own flesh will want to sit in sorrow and regret. However, the Savior died for all of our sins and He has given us power over sin in our lives. Beating ourselves up over the matter isn't taking ownership of the grace He gives us with regard to sin in our lives. Once you have let the Lord (and yourself) provide forgiveness, you won't experience any more sorrow, guilt or regret about your sin.

Forgive others and forgive God – The best way to move on is to forgive others and God in your heart and mind. Ask the Lord to fully forgive someone who has hurt you and put all of the bitterness or resentment towards the person(s) and/or God out of your mind. Doing this will allow you to move on from this difficult stage and to experience the peace of the Holy Spirit.

After the acceptance and resolution of the issues surrounding bitterness or resentment, Stage One is to be addressed.

Chapter 3

Stage Three:
The Buildup of Anger

Ephesians 4:26–27 declares, *"Be ye angry, and sin not: let not the sun go down upon your wrath: Neither give place to the devil."*

The inability to own and deal with bitterness or resentment leads to the third stage. In the "Ryrie Study Notes," Dr. Charles Ryrie describes Ephesians 4:26-27 as "... an anger that is not sinful, but even this must not be allowed to stay and fester and give the devil an opportunity."

The Wycliffe Bible Commentary talks about Ephesians 4:26 in this way. "Be ye angry, and sin not' ... there is such a thing as righteous anger, although the term is much abused. The apostle is saying that if you are angry, be sure it is the kind of anger that is not sinful. 'Let not the sun go down' ... even a righteous wrath by overindulgence may pass all too easily into sin" (Salmond).

There is a righteous anger and a righteous wrath, but both are on the "edge of a cliff." One's anger can build up into a righteous angry wrath without being sinful, but sin can come into this situation very easily because of the intensity of the individual's emotions. Of all the so-called negative human emotions, anger is the deepest and strongest; an explosive emotion. During this stage, if anger is not expressed righteously, it will deepen and strengthen and creates an opening for the devil. This opening is for a new anger that can be termed "unrighteous angry wrath" (or normal Biblical wrath). This opening for the devil puts Christians into the bondage of unrighteous angry wrath. Remember that at this stage there still can be the existence of righteous anger even after the Christian experiences the sins of bitterness or resentment.

It seems that God, in His grace, gives us one last chance to be angry in a non-sinning way; one last "easier" chance to go back to the heart of the problem by "dumping out" all the righteous anger. This includes dealing with unrighteous bitterness or resentment, to then be able to take aim on hurt and anxiety.

OVERCOMING STAGE THREE

Fully feel the righteous anger – It is important to understand that this should be in short duration because it is very easy to allow righteous anger to turn into unrighteous anger. Avoid, at all cost, the temptation to allow the sun to go down on your righteous anger. Depend on the Holy Spirit and draw close to the Lord for strength.

A great analogy for dealing with one's righteous anger is replacing a newly burned out light bulb. The light bulb and its heat represent your righteous anger. Your hand touching the hot light bulb represents your will or your decision to feel your righteous anger. Like with your righteous anger, your hand cannot stay on that hot bulb for too long. You need to turn that hot bulb in increments. Eventually, the hot bulb cools, and you can remove it. Removing the bulb represents the end of one's righteous anger. With this analogy in mind, feel your righteous anger in short increments, like your hand with that hot light bulb. Your righteous anger will begin to diminish in its energy like the cooled bulb.

Be swift to hear God (James 1:19-20) – When we are dealing with the issue of righteous anger, we need to understand what God is telling us. We can do that more easily when we are swifter to hear Him and slower to speak to Him.

Know anger's place – Accept firmly in your heart and mind that there is no existence and place for unrighteous anger in the Christian life.

Forgive – Forgiveness softens an angry heart.

After the acceptance and resolution of the issues surrounding unrighteous anger, all previous stages are to be addressed.

Chapter 4

Stage Four:
Malice or Wrath
(A State of Rejection)

Undiffused unrighteous anger deepens and strengthens and inevitably leads to the fourth stage. The floodgates to sin open to malice or unrighteous wrath. What had once begun as a possible non-sinning experience can now become incredibly sinful. The individual in stage four has entered the instability and torment of a double life or a double mind, becoming unstable in all their ways (James 1:8). This enormous amount of instability will add fuel to the fire of their malice and unrighteous wrath and open them up to a very brutal and fierce unchristian lifestyle. These two emotions can occur together, but for the sake of specificity we will look at them separately.

Malice

Titus 3:3 states, *"For we ourselves also were sometimes foolish, disobedient, deceived, serving divers lusts and pleasures, living in malice and envy, hateful, hating one another."*

We look to the *New Unger's Bible Dictionary* for a definition of malice:

> "Greek , "badness," 1 Corinthians 5:8; Ephesians 4:31; Colossians 3:8; Titus 3:3; 1 Peter 2:1. This Greek word denotes a vicious disposition, evilness, or wickedness. A kindred word is in Romans 1:29 (Greek , "bad character"), given by Paul in his long list of Gentile sins and implying malignant subtlety or malicious craftiness. Aristotle defines malice as "taking all things in the evil part" (2.13), as the Geneva version of the Scriptures likewise

renders it. It is "that peculiar form of evil which manifests itself in a malignant interpretation of the actions of others, an attributing of them all to the worst motive" (Trench, of the NT, p. 11)."

The primary problem with malice (and unrighteous wrath, as well) is that the individual is in a state of rejection toward just about everyone. This means that the wayward Christian is quick to brutally mistrust, question and misinterpret the motives of others. They are in direct opposition to Christian love. In fact, someone who is living a lifestyle of malice will be very prone to hurting someone else rather than loving them. This attitude can be hidden, to some extent, with regard to malice; however, it usually is too strong and will surface for others to see. This person will drive others away and put themselves in an increasingly isolated and lonely social position.

Unrighteous Wrath
The Strong's Talking Greek and Hebrew Dictionary defines normal Biblical wrath this way:

> "orgé from (oregomai); properly *desire* (as a *reaching* forth or *excitement* of the mind), i.e. (by analogy) violent *passion* (*ire,* or [justifiable] *abhorrence*); by implication *punishment*: anger, indignation, vengeance, wrath."

When someone is involved in a lifestyle of unrighteous wrath they are eyeball-high in evil. There is an elevation of energy in the mind that is fixated and focused on violent passion, punishment and vengeance. Like with malice, the person involved in unrighteous wrath is in total rejection of just about everyone. Although they may be able to hide their malice on a certain level, they will have a much more difficult time hiding their unrighteous wrath and their state of rejection because of the heightened energy in their mind. They will also have an overwhelming tendency to hurt others and drive others from them, putting themselves in an increasingly isolated and lonely social position (James 1:19-20).

It is important to recognize that unrighteous wrath leads to unrighteous living. A Christian cannot compartmentalize their unrighteous wrath from the rest of their Christian life. Believe it or not, a Christian can pull out of this rather quickly if they get on top of it quickly. However, for many it is not a quick process because of the heavy darkness of evil and the negativity that can easily consume them.

OVERCOMING STAGE FOUR

Take ownership of it – You must admit you are destroying your life with malice and unrighteous wrath and are not living a Christian lifestyle. Once this has been accomplished, avoid (at all costs) going back into the bondage of malice or unrighteous wrath.

Confess the sin of malice or unrighteous wrath to the Lord – An individual who has reached this stage has reached a very dark and deeply emotional and negative experience. They need to thoroughly depend on the Holy Spirit, and draw relationally close to the Lord Jesus along the way to full healing.

Forgive yourself for being controlled by malice and unrighteous wrath – This will not be easy, but is absolutely essential if there is going to be the possibility of moving on from this stage and dealing with the previous stages that have passed. It will not be easy, in large part, because you will now be able to see how far down you have fallen and to objectively see the horrible difficulty you are in.

Avoid self-hatred and hopelessness – It is essential to avoid these like the plague because you need to be your own best friend and not your own worst enemy. There may be ongoing tendencies to feel like you will never get out of this situation or to think that you are a lost cause. This negativity will destroy your restoration as a wonderful Christian servant.

Avoid thinking medication will fix everything – Even if you do take psychopharmacological medication, things will certainly not be fine immediately. Tell yourself that you are going to fight for your life and reestablish your Christian life and love with God.

Avoid ongoing battles with the devil – Satan will attempt to dominate stage four like a ferocious storm in the sky because your life has opened up to him. As a consequence, Satan's mighty power will be on display as he seeks to destroy your life. The best thing to do is to cast him out. A simple, "Get thee behind me, Satan. I cast thee out in the power of Jesus" is a good start and should be done several times. This is because Satan may have a special confidence during a Christian's weakened and insecure state. He is a bully and he loves to hit us when we are down. He is the ultimate cheap shot artist. If it takes 5, 10, 15, 20 or more times to cast him out than this is what is needed and when the devil has been cast out, put your mind on more positive and pleasant things. The devil will return, at a later time, to seek to torment anyone still in a weakened state. Avoid the fear of having to deal with Satan again by focusing on the positive and the pleasant while he's gone.

Plead with God the Father and the Lord Jesus to make the power of their presence known– Tap into the will of God. With all the darkness and negativity, there is a desperate need to sense the light and positive loving strength of God and Jesus. Jesus and the Holy Spirit will begin to minister in a dynamic way. For example, Jesus may flood or bombard your mind with positive thoughts and provide incredible peace during the ongoing storm.

Turn off your mind – At this stage, the mind is filled with excitement and energy, which makes the mind go very fast, and ultimately, will create a pattern of going very fast. The longer you are in the pattern of malice and unrighteous wrath the harder it will be to slow down the mind. That is why it is very important to get out of the malice and unrighteous wrath as soon as possible. Some of the best ways to turn off the mind is to get out of the house and focus on nature, listen to relaxing music and look to small blessings in life rather than big blessings. When we look for big blessings we don't appreciate the many small blessings that we have.

After the acceptance and resolution of the issues surrounding malice and unrighteous wrath, all previous stages are to be addressed.

Chapter 5

Stage Five:
Guilt (Guilt from Sin
of Malice and/or
Unrighteous Wrath)

The Apostle Paul in 1 Corinthians 11:31-32 says, *"For if we would judge ourselves, we should not be judged. But when we are judged, we are chastened of the Lord, that we should not be condemned with the world."*

The inability to accept and deal with malice and/or unrighteous wrath leads to the Fifth Stage. When someone has avoided dealing with their sinful behavior, it is only a matter of time until a powerfully intense and unwavering sense of guilt (Biblical shame) begins to convict them. This feeling of guilt is an act of love that Jesus is bringing the Christian individual. Jesus is doing this to chasten the Christian for the straying and sinning. Believe it or not, Jesus is trying to protect the person from condemnation with the world.

He is like the dad who has to bring out the rod against his misbehaving two-year-old. As the *Strong's* definition reveals, it is a rod that includes education, discipline/punishment, and instruction, learning and teaching. The *Strong's Talking Greek and Hebrew Dictionary* defines **chasten** as the following: *"(pais); to **train** up a child, i.e. **educate**, or (by implication) **discipline** (by punishment) chasten (-ise), instruct, learn, teach."*

We know that a loving dad has to do this to get a child back on a good track. The dad is doing this out of love, so his child does not grow up without a conscience. In this case, Jesus bestows this intense feeling of guilt because the Christian has developed a bad conscience and has stopped holding onto his faith. Jesus seeks to restore the Christian's conscience because if you lose your good conscience, you are doomed for shipwreck in your life here on earth. This is what Paul was talking about in 1 Timothy 1:19 where he says, *"Holding faith, and a good conscience; which some having put away concerning faith have made shipwreck."*

However, it must be emphasized that Jesus has not left the Christian during this time of chastening. The Christian has left Jesus by walking away into a double-life/double-mind of malice and unrighteous wrath. Jesus is still inside every Christian, but because of a sinful lifestyle, His love must now take on the forms of judgment, discipline and teaching. The Bible is clear on eternal security of one's salvation in Jesus Christ. Indeed, once saved forever saved.

OVERCOMING STAGE FIVE

Take ownership of the guilt – Feel, understand and accept this guilt completely which the Lord Jesus is allowing you to experience.

Cry out to the Lord – With great remorse and repentance with regard to the sin of malice or unrighteous wrath, plead with the Lord that He may be mightily felt and experienced. Like a loving parent with a rebellious child He has both arms waiting for His beloved Christian child. His perfect love is the greatest thing one needs at this stage. His love can only come if there is confession and repentance of wrongdoing.

Hold on to your Christian faith – Return to the simple Christian faith that you probably long for during this dark and difficult time. Allow that faith and love for the Lord Jesus, God the Father and the Holy Spirit to consume your life. Replace destructive hatred with incredible love beyond knowledge.

Forgive yourself – Once He has forgiven you, avoid dwelling on the wrong. Once the Lord Jesus has fully forgiven someone it is imperative to move on in God the Father and the Lord Jesus' perfect grace. Turning malice or unrighteous wrath inward is not the answer. Self-hatred is a sin, just like hating others, only worse. It is a double axe of hatred: one of someone else and two is that someone who is hated is oneself.

Avoid ongoing battles with Satan – Because the door has been left wide open for him to enter, Satan will have all of his nasty tricks ready. Simply focus on what is needed to get back in the proper relationship of closeness with the Lord Jesus, honor and praise God the Father, and depend on the Holy Spirit. Focusing on what needs to be done to get better will help avoid focusing on the devil's despicable deeds.

The mind needs to be turned off – Redirect the mind from all negativity to simple, more positive things. Remember that the Lord understands that sometimes you need to focus on things other than Him.

After the acceptance and resolution of the issues surrounding guilt, all previous stages are to be addressed.

Chapter 6

Stage Six:
Anxiety
(A Second Anxiety)

The inability to face guilt leads to the Sixth Stage. In fact, unless you have progressed to further stages it may be best not to continue reading past this stage. The person that has entered stage six or later needs to understand the overwhelming need to become involved in a quality Christ-centered Christian counseling situation.

As you may recall, the first anxiety is in Stage One. This second anxiety is at least twice as powerful than the first. A Christian cannot live in a pattern of guilt like the one in stage five, because the guilt is much too powerful to allow them to do so. That guilt quickly ushers them into a pattern of life that is extreme in its anxiety. This anxiety includes the previous stages that have piled up and given incredible expanse and intensity to one's inner turmoil. This stage can additionally include but is not limited to the following:

- General and incredible fear of the worst.
- Incredible insecurity and the anxiety of oneself and others. This includes the fear that the person is going to have a mental/nervous breakdown, and that they are too far gone to be helped.
- Incredible anxiety of harming oneself or someone else.
- Unreal incredible fear of specific things, specific situations or circumstances.
- An isolated panic attack or multiple panic attacks.
- Difficulty sleeping at night. One may only get two to four hours of sleep a night.

- A very fast-moving mind. This makes it extremely difficult to control the mind.
- Specific or general feelings of horrifying dread.

OVERCOMING STAGE SIX

A Quality Christ-Centered Counselor

A quality Jesus Christ-centered counselor (this would include psychologists, psychotherapists and appropriately trained pastors) are empowered to do the following very effectively:

1. Help you develop the following pattern:

   a) Be fully dependent on the Holy Spirit.

   b) Be relationally close with the Lord Jesus.

   c) Honor, glorify, praise and thank God.

2. Identify and express your emotions.

3. Identify and come to grips with any background issues.

4. Help you forgive whomever you need to forgive, including yourself.

5. Help you learn to love yourself.

6. Suggest selective and limited Biblical verses to apply to your life. It is also good to have general Bible reading for at least 30 minutes a day.

7. Help you to accept where you are at this time.

8. Help you understand that this whole situation may have started without sin on your part, but it has now escalated to include sin.

OTHER WAYS TO OVERCOME STAGE SIX

Talk with your medical doctor and counselor – Talk about the use of acetaminophen or a low-level anti-anxiety medication. Often, a basic low level potency medication can be effective for slowing down one's mind and helping one get additional sleep. When the mind races or does not get enough sleep during this stage it tends to go even faster and it becomes difficult for one to control their thoughts effectively. At this point, there is still a possibility of not needing major psychopharmacological medication. In fact, many times taking psychopharmacological medication, even at this stage, can give someone even more belief they are doomed. You still have plenty of hope of recovery in this stage.

Doubt is out – Don't give up. There is no place for this kind of thinking in this stage.

Accept changes – If you are having difficulty sleeping even with medication, remember that the lack of sleep is not going to be the final issue to ruin you. Remember, in wartime many soldiers are sleep-deprived and yet are still able to function at very high levels. The Holy Spirit will give you adequate energy to deal with this difficult time.

Own what John is saying – 1 John 4:18: *"There is no fear in love; but perfect love casteth out fear: because fear hath torment. He that feareth is not made perfect in love."*

After the acceptance and resolution of the issues surrounding anxiety, all previous stages are to be addressed.

Chapter 7

Stage Seven: Depression

The inability to take ownership and resolve the second anxiety leads to depression. Although the severity of depression can vary from better to worse, the best (less worse) experience of depression is still quite horrible.

THE NEED FOR PSYCHOPHARMACOLOGICAL MEDICATIONS

At this point, it is important to look at the possible need for psychopharmacological medication. If you fall into depression before your mid-to-late 30s, you have a very good chance of getting out of it without the use of psychopharmacological medication. However, this also means that an individual going through a depression after their mid-to-late 30s runs a serious risk of having to be on psychopharmacological medication for the rest of their lives.

This is because the human brain naturally gets older as we live longer, and cannot handle the stress and the emotional overload that it could when we were younger. Natural remedies may help in getting beyond depression, but there is no guarantee with natural remedies.

THE INDIVIDUAL IN STAGE SEVEN

The following is a description of a person who is going through depression. Depression can include, but is not limited to the following:

- A very difficult time sleeping at night or a pattern of sleeping too much at night.
- A horrifying feeling or sense of darkness or blackness.
- Thoughts and feelings of extreme negativity.

- A very fast-moving mind or a very slow-moving mind.
- Occasional or frequent bouts of intense crying. This comes from a beyond-belief sense of sadness.

OVERCOMING STAGE SEVEN

If you haven't already, talk to your doctor – Talk with your medical doctor and/or Christ-centered counselor about the use of acetaminophen or other low-level medications.

Include more counseling – Be open with your Christ-centered counselor about attending two therapeutic hours of counseling every week.

Live a normal schedule – This will give you the confidence that you are not too far gone, even if you believe you are. It will also give a sense of positive accomplishment.

One day at a time – At all costs, seek to live one day, one hour or one moment at a time. Often, a depressed person's vision of even tomorrow is extremely negative.

After the acceptance and resolution of the issues surrounding depression, all previous stages are to be addressed.

Chapter 8

Stage Eight:
Unreality

The cost is tragic if a person does not come to grips and deal with their depression. Stage eight is unreality and unreality can include but is not limited to the following:

1. High powered and frequent imaginations of things which are not real - The individual owns the belief that these imaginations are a part of reality.

2. Possible physiological thoughts of the unreal - One may experience biological thoughts of the unreal as very real. In other words, they may experience hallucinations as a part of reality.

3. The person may experience unnatural high levels of energy and euphoria followed by unnatural low levels of energy and depression.

4. The individual may experience depression like that in Stage Seven, or worse.

OVERCOMING STAGE EIGHT

When it comes to acceptance and working through this stage, the practical helping items here are similar to the many earlier. Here are some additions:

There is an increased need for medication – This stage is still not a guarantee that you need to be on psychopharmacological medication, however, the need for it at this stage has increased radically.

Increased access to your counselor – Again, attending at least two therapeutic counseling hours with your Christ-centered counselor is crucial. In addition, you need to be able to call your counselor if you are experiencing a serious crisis.

Avoid the great temptation to pull away from social situations – One seriously needs human contact with Christian love at this time.

After the acceptance and resolution of the issues surrounding unreality, all previous stages are to be addressed.

Chapter 9

Stage Nine:
Escape or Suicide

The inability to take ownership and deal with unreality leads to the Ninth Stage, which becomes the end of the line. Humans were not created to handle the build-up of the first eight stages. This build-up leads to escape or suicide. Due to this, the need for major psychopharmacological medication at this point becomes overwhelming.

One cannot stay in this stage long before the overwhelming desire or perceived need for escape or suicide fully dominates and controls his life. Escape may include but is not limited to the following:

- Suicide
- The consistent and/or heavy use of substances (drugs).
- Running away from home.
- Horrible physiological abnormalities as a consequence of escaping.
- Any variety of major psychiatric abnormalities as a consequence of escaping.

OVERCOMING STAGE NINE

Increase your counseling time – You will need to attend hour-long therapeutic sessions at least three times a week and be able to call your counselor during times of crisis.

Acting quickly – You must act fast on the advice of a Christ-centered counselor on how to get out of this stage as quickly as possible.

Keep in touch – Avoid escaping from socialization and keep in touch with loving Christians.

Hang on – Never give up on life. Never!

After the acceptance and resolution of the issues surrounding escape or suicide, all previous stages are to be addressed. The inability to take ownership and deal with the issues involved in Stage Nine will lead to suicide or the permanent effects from escape, which would include psychiatric care, on some level, for the rest of one's life.

Bibliography

Holy Bible. *King James Version*. Database WORDsearch Corp., 2007.

New Unger's Bible Dictionary, The. Unger, Merrill F. Chicago, Illinois: Moody Press of Chicago, 1988. Database WORDsearch Corp., 2003.

Ryrie Study Notes. Ryrie, Charles Caldwell. Chicago: The Moody Bible Institute of Chicago, 1986, 1995. Database WORDsearch Corp., 2004.

Strong's Concordance, Strong, James. Text and Database WORDsearch Corp., 2007.

Strong's Talking Greek and Hebrew Dictionary. Strong, James. Text and Database WORDsearch Corp., 2007.

Wycliffe Bible Commentary, The. Pfeiffer, Charles F. and Harrison, Everett F. Chicago: The Moody Bible Institute of Chicago, 1962, 1990. Database WORDsearch Corp, 2008.

Other Suggested Resources

1918. Database WORDsearch Corp., 2008.

Holy Spirit, The. Ryrie, Charles C. 1965, 1997 Database WORDsearch Corp., 2006.

Strong's Concordance, Strong, James. Text and Database WORDsearch Corp., 2007.

Legal Statements/ Disclaimer

1. Howard Blandau authorized me to receive and take ownership of all benefits (including financial) that result from the use of his insights, thoughts, ideas, etc. This includes this book entitled *LifeSights: Book One*, or any other written material, presented material, or production of any sort, which are the individual, combined and/or unified insights, thoughts or ideas of Howard Blandau and/or T. George Homsher.

2. A number of headings or statements that are made in this book, and the books to come, are those that I remember from speaking with Howard Blandau. I am unable to distinguish which headings or statements are his and which headings or statements could have been quoted from someone else. If any stated quotes or thoughts are from someone else originally, the author greatly apologizes. Evidence of this occurring would greatly be appreciated and upon the analysis of this evidence, if a mistake has been made, I will either identify the authors of the stated quotes or thoughts and/or will reword them in a later edition.

3. This book in no way is intended to be used to diagnose, treat, or cure any specific individual problem(s). Individuals are highly recommended to see a qualified Helping Professional and Medical Doctor to help them diagnose, treat, and/or cure their own specified problem(s).